I0818549

WNBA
SEATTLE STORM
Mitchell Lane
PUBLISHERS
Carla Mooney

Mitchell Lane
PUBLISHERS

mitchelllanepub.com

2001 SW 31st Avenue
Hallandale, FL 33009

First Edition, 2026.
Author: Carla Mooney
Designer: Ed Morgan
Editor: Tammy Gagne

Series: WNBA
Title: Seattle Storm

Library bound ISBN: 979-8-89260-485-7
eBook ISBN: 979-8-89260-487-1

Photo credits: p. 11 sportslogos.net; balance Alamy

CONTENTS

Chapter ONE

CHAMPIONS AGAIN

The COVID-19 **pandemic** shut down much of the world for months in 2020. But nothing could stop the Seattle Storm that year. To save the season, the Women's National Basketball Association (WNBA) set up a bubble environment in Florida and cut the games back to twenty-two.

CHAPTER ONE

Despite the unusual situation, the Storm thrived. The team tied the Las Vegas Aces for the best regular season record with 18 wins and 4 losses. That record earned the Storm a bye, which allowed them to automatically advance to the semifinals. In the semifinals, the Storm swept the Minnesota Lynx in three games.

In the finals, the Storm faced the Las Vegas Aces. Led by All-Star players Sue Bird and Breanna Stewart, the Storm dominated the play. In game one, Bird set a playoff record with 16 **assists**. Stewart scored 37 points, which was the second-best in WNBA Finals history. In game two, the Storm players set another finals record for assists. The Seattle team led the best-of-five series 2–0.

Champions Again

Forward Sue Bird warms up with a basketball before a Seattle Storm game.

CHAPTER ONE

The Storm didn't let up in game three. They won 92–59 to clinch the title and sweep the series. Their 33-point win was the largest **margin** of victory in WNBA Finals history. The title was the Storm's fourth championship. The team was now tied with the Minnesota Lynx and Houston Comets for the most WNBA titles.

Breanna Stewart talked about how the Storm dealt with the trials of the 2020 season. "I think the greatest challenge was just all the **adversity**. Everybody bought in. We're a chill team, and we kind of rolled with the punches and continued to do what we do. Now we're the champs," she said in an interview on ESPN.

Champions Again

Center Ezi Magbegor drives the ball down the court during a 2024 game against the Dallas Wings.

FAST FACT

As of 2024, the Storm has never lost a WNBA Final.

Chapter TWO

FROM LAST TO FIRST

The Storm's original logo from 2000 featured the Space Needle.

In 2000, the WNBA added four new teams to the league. One team was the Seattle Storm. The Storm play in Seattle, Washington. They are part of the WNBA's Western Conference. The team's name was chosen as a nod to Seattle's rainy climate.

CHAPTER TWO

In its first season, the Storm finished in last place. Their record was 6–26. Over the next few seasons, the team steadily improved. In 2001, the Storm **drafted** Lauren Jackson. A year later, they added Sue Bird. Jackson and Bird led the team to the 2004 WNBA Finals. The Storm won its first championship title that year, beating the Connecticut Sun.

Over the next fifteen years, the Storm was a **consistent** playoff team. Its players swept the Atlanta Dream 3–0 to win their second WNBA title in 2010. In 2016, the Storm drafted **forward** Breanna Stewart with the first overall pick. She quickly became a star on the court. She helped lead the Storm to two more WNBA titles, in 2018 and 2020.

From Last to First

All-star forward Sue Bird won a gold medal with the U.S. women's basketball team at the 2012 London Olympics.

FAST FACT

The Storm is owned by Force 10 Hoops, a group of three Seattle businesswomen who bought the team in 2008 to keep it in Seattle. In 2024, Sue Bird, who retired from the WNBA in 2022, joined the Storm's ownership group.

CHAPTER TWO

The Storm play at Climate Pledge Arena in Seattle. Their games are known for a family-friendly setting. Doppler, the team **mascot**, entertains fans throughout the games. The all-kid Seattle Storm Dance Troupe performs during halftime and other breaks in the game. Star player Jewell Loyd talked about the atmosphere at Storm home games. "Our Storm fans always come out and support us and so we definitely appreciate it," she told *The Next* website.

From Last to First

Doppler energizes the crowd at each Seattle Storm game, connecting with fans of all ages.

Chapter THREE

GUIDING THE STORM

Lin Dunn, the Storm's first head coach and manager

The Seattle Storm has had several head coaches. Lin Dunn was the Storm's first head coach and general manager. Dunn had previously been a successful college basketball coach. She laid the foundation for the Storm from 2000 to 2002. Dunn drafted key Storm players such as Sue Bird.

CHAPTER THREE

Coach Anne Donovan followed Dunn in 2003. As a player, Donovan had led the U.S. women to gold medals at the 1984 and 1988 Olympics. After retiring as a player, Donovan coached college teams. She also coached in the American Basketball League, a women's league that operated from 1996 to 1998. After joining the Storm, Donovan led the team to its first WNBA title in 2004. A series of coaches followed Donovan, including Brian Agler and Dan Hughes.

In 2021, the Storm named Noelle Quinn as the team's head coach. She played in the WNBA for twelve years. In 2018, she won a WNBA championship with the Storm. Quinn retired from playing in 2019 and joined the Storm as an assistant coach before moving into the role of head coach.

Guiding the Storm

Anne Donovan huddles with Storm players during a time-out in 2004.

CHAPTER THREE

Storm general manager Talisa Rhea talked about Quinn in a 2023 press release. "Noelle's competitive passion, basketball [knowledge], and extensive playing career, coupled with her sideline experience as one of the longest-**tenured** coaches in the league, positions our team to be successful as we pursue excellence on the court," said Rhea.

Quinn led the Storm to the playoffs in 2021 and 2022. Quinn has talked about being a Black female head coach in the WNBA in a 2021 news conference. She gave credit to the Black women who had come before her. "They crawled so I could walk. I sit on those shoulders. For me, it's important that I'm not a woman, I'm a Black woman. . . . There is value in that. My experience is in that. It has shaped me, and it has molded me, and that is who I am," she said.

Guiding the Storm

FAST FACT

Head Coach Noelle Quinn was one of three Black head coaches in the WNBA for the 2024 season.

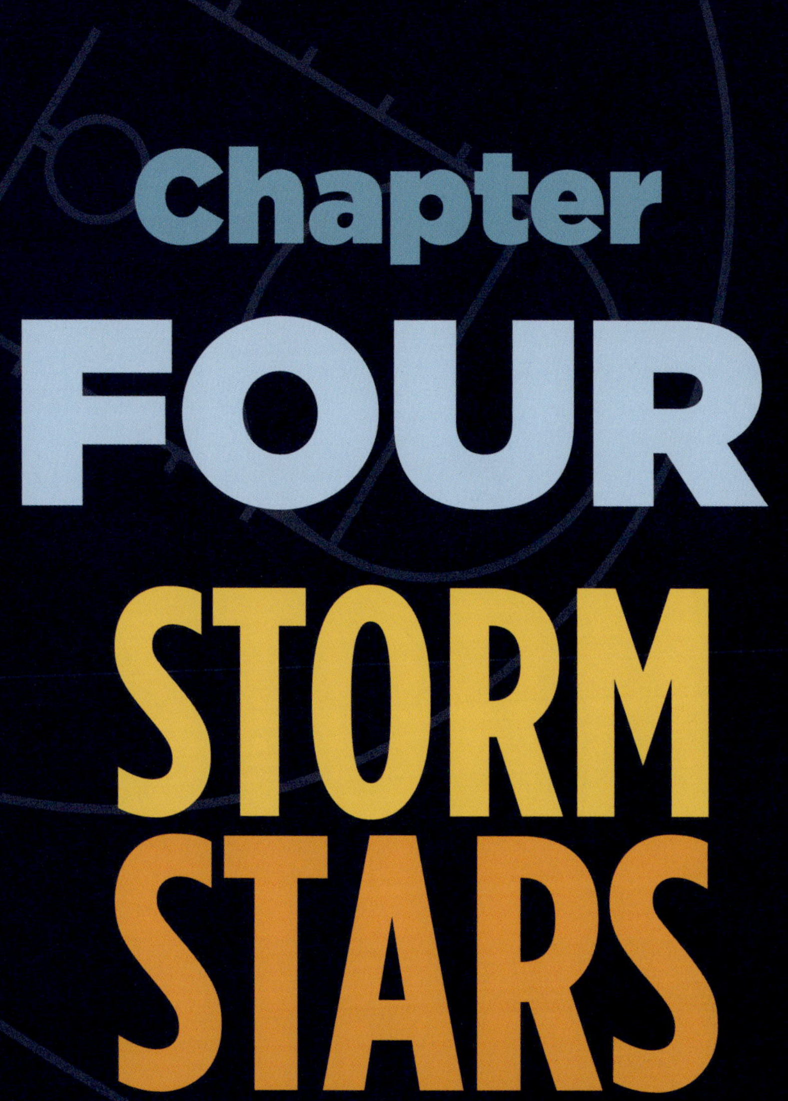

Chapter FOUR

STORM STARS

Storm guard Jewell Loyd looks for an open shot during a game against the Chicago Sky in 2022.

One of the Storm's top performers was **guard** Jewell Loyd. Chosen by Seattle as the first overall pick in the draft, Loyd was named the WNBA **Rookie** of the Year in 2015. She won two championships with the Storm, in 2018 and 2020. Loyd was selected as a WNBA All-Star for the sixth time in 2024. She was traded to the Las Vegas Aces before the 2025 season.

CHAPTER FOUR

Coach Noelle Quinn discussed Loyd in a 2023 press release. "Jewell brings a level of excellence to our team on the court and consistently proves that she is one of the best in our league. . . . She is our leader and someone that we look forward to locking arms with heading into this new era of Storm basketball," Quinn said.

Nneka Ogwumike joined the Storm as a **free agent** in 2024. She is a nine-time WNBA All-Star and the league's 2016 Most Valuable Player (MVP). As a forward, Ogwumike is one of the WNBA's top offensive players. She has been among the top thirty players in scoring during her twelve seasons in the league. In the 2024 season, Ogwumike was the Storm's second-leading scorer through twenty-five games. She averaged nearly 18 points per game.

FAST FACT

Jewell Loyd is also known as the Gold Mamba, a nickname given to her by the late basketball star Kobe Bryant.

CHAPTER FOUR

In August 2024, forward Gabby Williams rejoined the Storm after playing for the team in 2022. She missed the beginning of the WNBA season to train with the French national team for the Paris Olympics. At the Olympics, Williams led France to a silver medal. She was named the Best Defensive Player at the Paris Games. After the 2024 season, Williams left the Storm to play in Europe.

The Seattle Storm has a long history of winning. Over the years, the team has had many memorable moments and players. With star athletes such as Loyd, Ogwumike, and Williams, the Storm hopes to rise to the league's summit again in the future.

Storm Stars

Forward Gabby Williams dribbles down the court during a game against the Dallas Wings in 2024.

GLOSSARY

adversity
Great difficulty

assists
Passes made to teammates, which lead to scored points

consistent
Dependable in performance regardless of the opponent or situation

drafted
Selected to join a team

forward
A basketball player who plays near the basket, often rebounding and scoring points

free agent
A player who is free to sign a contract with any team

guard
A basketball player who focuses on passing, dribbling, and setting up plays

margin
The difference between two numbers

mascot
An animal or character that represents a group

pandemic
A disease outbreak occurring over a wide geographical area

rookie
An athlete playing her first season as a member of a professional sports team

tenured
Having served in a job or position

SLAM DUNK WNBA TRIVIA

- The Storm's theme song is "Thunderstruck" by AC/DC. The song can be heard as the players are introduced at each game.
- The team's newsletter is called the *StormWatch*.
- The Storm won the WNBA's first Commissioner's Cup in 2021. This tournament now takes place each year during the regular season.
- Jewell Loyd was named the MVP of the 2024 All-Star Game after scoring a record 31 points.
- Nneka Ogwumike is one of sixteen players in WNBA history to score at least 5,800 career points.
- The Seattle Sports Commission named Jewell Loyd the Women's Sports Star of the Year in 2024.

FIND OUT MORE

IN PRINT

Fredeen, Kerry Kelaher. *Las Vegas Aces*. Mitchell Lane Publishers, 2026.

Hill, Anne E. *Inside the Seattle Storm*. Lerner Publications, 2023.

O'Neal, Ciara. *The WNBA Finals*. Apex, 2023.

ON THE INTERNET

Seattle Storm.
https://storm.wnba.com.

"Seattle Storm," ***ESPN*, n.d.**
www.espn.com/wnba/team/_/name/sea/seattle-storm.

"Seattle Storm," ***FOX Sports*, n.d.**
www.foxsports.com/wnba/seattle-storm-team.

INDEX

About the Author

Carla Mooney is the author of many books for young adults and children. She lives in Pittsburgh, Pennsylvania, with her husband and three children. She enjoys watching all types of sports, including women's basketball.